ALL ABOUT LOVE

illustrated by Richard Max Kolding

The Standard Publishing Company, Cincinnati, Ohio. A division of Standex International Corporation.
© 1997 by The Standard Publishing Company. Printed in the United States of America.
ISBN 0-7847-0603-4. All rights reserved. Designed by Coleen Davis.

Love is patient.

1 Corinthians 13:4

Love is kind.

1 Corinthians 13:4

"Love your neighbor as yourself."

Matthew 22:39

Do everything in love.

1 Corinthians 16:14

Love the Lord your God
with all your heart.

Matthew 22:37

Your love has given me great joy.

Philemon 1:7

I will sing of your love.
Psalm 101:1

Above all, love each other.

1 Peter 4:8

The Lord watches over all who love him.

Psalm 145:20

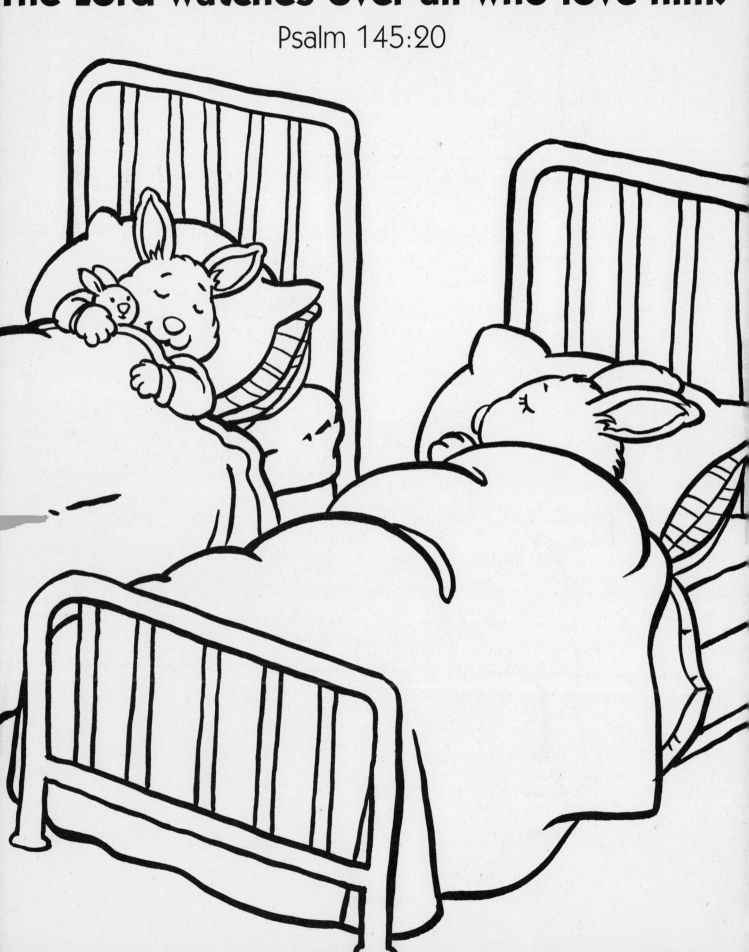

I will be glad and rejoice in your love.

Psalm 31:7

God is love.

1 John 4:8